# Visible Music

# By

# Martyn Halsall

First Edition: Visible Music by Martyn Halsall

ISBN: 978 1 9163881 1 6

First published in the UK in 2020 by Caldew Press.

Caldew Press
Tolivar
12 St George's Crescent
Carlisle
CA3 9NL

caldew-press@outlook.com
www.caldewpress.com

CALDEW PRESS

For all who experience cancer.

# Contents

# Visible Music

## Balmacqueen

Gnarlings of rocks, salt stream, thin gruel of peatland,
not even an agreed name: three possible spellings
identify the village, hamlet, township
scattered through crofts between Skye's ridge and coastline.

This cottage, given to retreat, built into silence,
where prayer is often silence or overheard tide,
stands back, slightly above the tilt of pasture,
looking to where the Hebrides become horizon.

First warning, here; tautening of chest, a spasm,
sending me out to evening's clover breeze
running inland from machair, disputing quiet
lodged here for healing, under a chapel's skylight.

Next morning's so full of sky the room's lit blue;
whatever was sensed ascends larks' vertical scales.

## Holy Trinity Croft House

Turn left outdoors, as entering a Eucharist.
Morning is consecrated; tide, silvered chalice
as swilled by a priest's wrist, surf laced around her surplice.
High water, elevated, skids the island

where pain began, where many came for healing;
a sunlit cottage, shadowed by evening panelling.
Its chapel, with its one-armed crucifix,
held stories, written of costs, and restoration.

Afterwards, try to recall what made it blessed:
mist sheathing ridge, crumb-scatter of whitewashed crofts,
a curlew celebrating through its choir of moorland;
grey index finger profile, North, to Lewis.

All that was morning, breeze young as white hours.
Evening brought peeled-back, raw wound end of day;
bloodshot, scar tissue sky, a bandaged West;
and the woman, guardian of this house of prayer,
crossing low fields with her dogs for a conversation.

## Small Things

Catch in the throat, bowstring across the heart:
curry? The young doctor ventures "indigestion?".
Then notes repeat, repeat, repeat, and lifts the phone.

Fast-track, and so my phone call for delay
meets with professional brusqueness. That weekend
hesitancy over lunch; planned tests, procedures.

Small things: a diary note for evening tablets,
going out to gather last sweet peas from frames
wigwammed before diagnosis, noticing

each deepening crimson staining blackberry leaves,
the full moon winking as a wind stirs larch;
geese arrowing south before North winter comes.

# After Copernicus

You turn aside, daring barely a sideways glance
to the monitor showing red mass, funnelled pulsing.
It is your interior, resembling a distant star;
deep space that's rarely seen at this end of the visible.

I look away, then look to find it again
cosmic, as in a book review: Non-fiction;
swirl of fawn tissue round a molten heart
set in black velvet's cold, unreachable night-time.

Something Copernicus, in a Polish side-street,
dreamed of relating, eye to his telescope,
his finger pointing to nothing to identify
everything during last thirteen billion years,

and claim, although the nurses are all attention,
we are not the universe centre, yet are unique.
You hold what life remains. You feel alone.

## Leaving the Waiting Room

Same colour, texture as egg box, foggy grey
roughage of recycled card; a waiting room
to wait in till the dizzy world stops, and steadies.

Nurses disperse into the present tense
having warned: "It's not good news." after the scan,
having sat me still as the room began to sway,
left me with the egg box for turbulence, air-sickness.

Shapes were changing, crescent of a waning moon,
though morning remained sunlit. Walking across
the city found people full of self-important things,
like slipping out for a sandwich, buying cards.

We followed in their footsteps, think of labs
where others would analyse my interior findings
like reading a distant galaxy. Instead of rooms
we made our way to the coast, hoping for curlew.

## Drigg Sands

Tide had just turned; planed, widening sands
were spreading banquet for sanderling, ringed plover
peppering to tideline. Evening had tinted sky
orange over stillness. Flat water. Single waves
lazed ashore in reversing, quickening ebb.

Right place to come with love, and border collie
after those difficult words, oncology,
cannula, that prick of needle, sideways glances
showing pulsing crimson; my internal cosmos.

Possibly, and possibly not. They'd probe for answers:
'It's not good news', but there'd be checks, biopsy.
The beach was empty, like a blank manuscript.
Prelude was dark, black bunting of evening curlew
following this coast south; wild dusk in their music.

## Correspondences

Mid-winter: the morning train passes between
halts with their shower-rinsed platforms smelling of tide.

We travel under a Calvinist sky; thin creams over
greys, over Delft blue, stripped back to that high-minded
coming ashore, with rumours of the New World.

Ground falters, losing footing at cliff or dune;
starched ruffs of breakers pour parallel with ebb,
foreshore's adrift, sand ironed, scattered stone
smelted as sun breaks through like a revelation.

Wind cuts the coast where cormorants become
their own black crucifixions, drying wings.

Later, after visiting the oncology suite,
we return to our own indoors, and light a fire
against the darkening chill. Shadowed panelling
squares off the world. I imagine, in Protestant weather,

Rembrandt's black figures, clustered around a body
similar to mine laid on the procedure table;
or his late self-portrait, staring back in amazement.

I had sent you my news, of being a cancer patient.
Days passed without reply, question, reaction.

## Islanders

Shared memories come as forms of consolation:
a drinker's tractor angled to an Irish bar,
light redefining silence over an island,
white tip of shadow- all a sea eagle left,
political banter showered like confetti,
a haiku grace drawn into candlelight.

Advice, after the shock of diagnosis
to keep beliefs we might explore, not share.
You seem to mean the wounded hands of Christ
still beckoning in stained glass; your rear view mirror.

You say you are no typist, that  defining thoughts
elude the keys, not knowing what to say
about the news that comes across as silence
you hear sometimes as God, God's conversation.

So quick reply as you are about to leave.
(I also, in another sort of way?).
I'll look beyond the present tense, envisage
returning to an island where near sky
crashes ashore in cloud banks and barred lighting,
stepping in, layer by layer, from Atlantic.

## Marionette

Pouch of clear water yard above my forehead
drips through a green valve, pulsing to a plastic tumour
where tears pause, gather above a decanting vein,
a marionette string taped to my non-writing hand.

It enters my system through a white connection,
and cannula, piped, valved in two shades of blue.
System needs flushing before three drugs begin
the hard work of the night's counter-attack.

First morning of trench warfare, first overnight
to start the chemo sessions before the theatre.
Common vocabulary with theatre, someone
pulling strings; nurse, surgeon, puppet-master

encouraging the arm raised upwards in salute,
pulled taut, as also a gesture of submission.

## Baxter

Looking again I see the sac has turned
grey as raw slate, as angled as a shatter,
and labelled "Baxter" like round rampart apse
edging west fells around lanes veining Lamplugh.

Sole light seeps from the clipped, pale monitor's
counting-down screen, tunnel for transparent tubes
that feed dripped teardrops from a bag to hand,
keep everything in night-time silhouette.

Electrics shoot arrows across a small, black screen,
recording infusion at millilitres an hour.
The pouch deflates to old wineskin, collapsed lung,
ageing in draining, wrinkling in October sunlight

like hump and ramp that shapes the fell and shares
prospect with medicine. Promise before too long
we'll climb it, and see far if weather's clear:
summer time, some time later, "after all of this".

Look up again, and all the bags have flown,
leaving stand weathercock, without directions.

## Partings

Once hair lapped shoulders, sprang around my head
like a philosophy festival. Now, whatever's left
turns comb into a fieldmouse, the white sink
dark to Sargasso of elvers, leaving home.

Now mental landscape's pink, ears re-appear
after decades below waves, as undertones.
Sideboards chopped as tree stumps have clung on
mossed as rumours of felling through ancient woodland.

Predecessors from the other end of chemotherapy
and surgery forecast it will return. "Watch out," they say,
"for the first stubble sprouts across  your head.

"Meanwhile, it will still be you." (In a flesh-coloured helmet).
I keep thoughts warm with a football fan's red beanie,
this morning admiring late golds, seeping through woodland.

## Becoming my Father

Friends asked, in a post-war classroom. about our fathers.
One said his was the first to cross the Rhine-
a little man, a tall war-hero to him.

Another said his father, when a policeman,
had help to arrest a murderer after dark,
possibly twilight; often twilight then.

War only stretched to Midlands for my father,
who only saw a policeman on point duty,
whom I recall most lately for his thinnings.

Not just his hair, to bare a sort of tonsure,
but his whole frame, shrinkage and drawing back,
body, like mind, into a reticence.

That same pattern of hair, thinning to shine,
and body losing mass to make stick fencing
I saw in you, and now the mirror frames.

# Kop

Later in his life my grandfather followed
"In the Footsteps of Jesus" on a package tour
to Israel, Holy Land to some, but first
he visited a local market for a shoulder bag.

A Leicester City supporter, if anyone's,
though preferring the slim willow,and long pitched boundary.
A stallholder foisted red plastic over his shoulder:
"Liverpool, wear this and you'll never walk alone,

"be one of the boys". His hopeful photos showed
some distant Dead Sea caves, a smudge
of camels, Temple Mount, and someone's finger
pointing to the Wailing Wall, and several churches.

Now that my hair has gone I remember him
as I reach for a beanie hat, egg cosy to baldness.
Claret, and a saggy fit for West Ham United,
bought as ironic gift by a season ticketer

before my hair thinned, and the nurses' verdict.
I sport it, with its sledge hammer and turrets badge,
as relevant as the Kop to Bethlehem
as I prune an apple tree, trying to remember his guidance.

## Seeds

I packet up some dozens as Christmas gifts,
nasturtium seeds, perhaps size of apprentice tumours,
but with no body surrounding or sustaining.

Each gifted different, micro-shaped lung or brain;
some smooth skull following chemo-therapy,
most ridged a furrow fawn, set down for planting.

Picture their destinations: one city garden
where they may wander a border, setting fire
to forbidding fencing, or extending edges of flower-bed;

one balcony where they can roam, cascade
orange and scarlet silence from gramophone horns
of flowers above the river, its meniscus skullers.

Some stretching, eased to sunlight, placed botanically
through landscaped rockery after ph readings,
sited according to the book, settled within budget.

We collected seeds green as they wandered over
remains of autumn towards a threat of frost;
dried them on yesterday's news as the boiler fired,

will plant our share for a fresh annualling of liana
empty clock face of leaves that bring the Claude Glass
to bear on shade, and vein after a shower

till a tilt of breeze brings watering from overturn.
Something to watch for, shoot, stream stretch, first flare
of flower and its promise, after the operation.

**Nasturtiums**
**(for Isobel)**

She loved nasturtiums, their tumbling cables, rambles,
aspiring beanstalks, radar saucer leaves
scanning sunlight, stars, becoming a priest's plant
disclosing heaven in the ordinary gardens.

Also a summer's listing; Golden Gleam
high yellow crag tops of a climbing morning;
Empress of India scarlets of mixed sunset,
or shepherds' warning within the Scarlet Gleam.

Off-colours of autumn, when she gathered seeds,
their ridges soft lime between finger and thumb
hardening to almost wood vein, varnishing,

drying to tumour, in the boiler room.
She'd plant them hard, then watch shoots softening
find angles under rain; hope for a flowering.

## Purchase

Bought just before sailing, small change cash and guilt,
Fisherman's jumper knitted for the charity shop
for wearing in this world's keen edge of weather,
and given for another world, without this rain,
or guarantees of safety, food and shelter.
Guilt comes from taking it, export, to comfort.

Same grey as winter sky, just before snow,
weight of the wind that drove sails out of Orkney
round islands down to mainland salted ages
ago, before cancer became a verdict.

I draw it out, run density of stitching
between finger and thumb, imagining
my need of it, drawn tired to a fireside,
recovering from one dose, steeled for the next
yet planning islands; stilled, but sailing in it.

## Airspace: Second Scan

Same soundtrack as air-travel, aerial breath
hisses, exhales, night flight that's windowless
but flat out, looking up; sentenced to stillness.

First, interview, perched on the bed you'll make
your own for an hour while the tracer finds
its way around your body; pipes, canals.

You listen to Brahms' sawn velvet violins,
wrapped in a gown, allowed to keep your socks
like those provided, first class, to Osaka.

Then ushered to the scanner, padded on
hard pillow like a neck brace, hands across
your chest as effigy of a medieval knight.

Ceiling is abstract art of bars and lights,
becoming snowfield through thousand feet of air,
pause; glide back through deep space. Quiet continents

may pass by either side. You would not know
or guess what they are seeing, finding, listing.
There is no time here, gradually you compose

meaning from light and steel abstraction, visit
empty beach, outlaws' wood, plan to return
by not daring to move, disturb the readings.

Eventually you emerge, are lowered, told
to rise again, led to a changing room;
told to have tea and biscuits before you leave,

imagining the images on their way
to make a case for treatment, or a verdict:
black nights, white dawn, interiors of stars.

## Memory from Skye

Way back, as if to township set on Skye:
left out of Larch Ward, past the nursing station,
along a gallery roofed by glass and cloud,
as seeking Skye beyond revolving doors,

and then, out. The world has been going on,
raining, and going to work, in conversation,
talking to itself, while I acquired new words
drip-fed through cannula, shod in surgical stockings

through night fractured by health checks, blood pressure
readings,
temperature taken by ear, as if hearing heat,
checking the heart; swallowing small tubs of tablets.

Imagine resuming the journey back, due North,
signpost to a strung-out township; walk last mile
returning, hoping still to hear those curlew.

# Shifts

Clusters of nuclear workers arc round train doors,
padded from walks through straight lines of the site,
past coils of razor wire, mesh fencing avenues,
discipline of concrete blocks, dusk coloured factories.

They arrived in half-light, shorelines being redefined
by channels, gantries, bridges; lamps squinting daylight.
To their west scrubland, shingle, shore, white uncurl
and pour of breakers; half-light of early swans.

Aboard now, stuffed compartments, same bowed heads
as miners coming up, out of dark to darkness
a generation since, same underground
but now a burial ground, a poisoning.

Same fashion for uniform, skull-capped wool hats,
dark jackets, yoke-shouldered with a powerful name,
flashes for catching light, rucksacks stacked fast
on racks; more checking screens than conversations.

Light; the site passes back, becomes a distant
mass picket of chimneys against the polished tide.
An oystercatcher seems to race the carriage,
gulls mass across the webs and drain of channels.

In all the stillness following the rattling train
dark work continues, mining by time and weather,
an unseen aftermath, plutonium stretch
from bombs to cancer patients among the passengers.

## Childs

Bravely she carried to the wedding her dead
child in a billow of dress that passed
for maternity smock, or a celebration of August.

Photos show her smiling, sitting on a tabled stone
honouring the dead. Between the laughter lines
a consciousness of a future not to be born,
echoes among ancient yews, and children's voices.

Growth also in the stomach, a tumour comes
unbidden, and unwanted child of fear,
possibly the same gestation, different words-
scans, chemo- pause until deep surgery

plots for a death with sharp hopes of fresh life.
Forty years on, beyond memory and death plot,
we see same smiles in faces of her three grown sons.

## Rests

Rest began as a gap on a chart between beats
being tapped, clashed, drummed out by percussionists
aged six, except for me who broke the silence,
turned red among sniggers, teacher's withering scorn.

Now more frequent demands, and always observed,
moving from bed to chair, table to fireside,
paper soon folding forwards, head tilting back
into doze; second hand turning unnoticed

as afternoon disappears. Whatever conferences,
machinations or disputes, councils of war
take place, I tender my apologies,

hoping when I wake to resume planning
for the eventual, and the ordinary; that small
blue bag of wood to be brought up from the shed.

## Wards

Like following penitents into a Catholic church
where they pause to sign in, with forefinger from standing
water;
an invisible cross from forehead down to heart,
just as we pause for hand-gel, entering the ward.

Same starting again with cleansing, aisles, waiting spaces
for equipment to enact the promised healing,
everything mobile; steel trees for feeds and drips,
spare beds, like that once let down through a ceiling.

Same sense of chapel in hospital weekends,
same emptiness that fills so many churches,
same evidence of people having left,
long wait through vacant space without responses.

Leaving, you cup your hand, as for a wafer,
squeeze briefly with the middle or trigger finger,
releasing foam, or gel, sea's edge, ebbed blessing
that even in emptiness brings absolution.

## Bloods

Hope with this bloodshed that the count is high
enough to guarantee continuing treatment.
Warning of a sharp scratch after raising vein
as needle bayonet's held while a phial's screwed
to drain red with the drawing of the syringe.
Two capsules labelled, sent away for tests,
dispatched with all the urgency of a campaign.

We wander down the valley to the shelter,
granite and slate, benched seats, no list of Fallen
here just a refuge out of wind. A shower passes,
baptism for today's eleventh hour
this grey eleventh day. Two priests, two wreaths,
thin wind in trees breaks silence; crags
are rinsed with clouds as famous words are said.

No narrow nations; wide plaque remembers all
who fell wherever "patriot" was defined
as living land, wherever strong wind rang-
woods or cleared barraged cloud off steep or height.
We turn home down the one road veining valley,
imagine someone with a microscope,
a smear of blood, a verdict over treatment.

## Times

Three: collie takes off, as from ballista,
white streak on beach, deft turn to field his ball,
circle of sweep to return; his whole world
speed. I follow on footsteps slowed by chemo.

Four: mornings awake, edging light's tideline
as alone on endless sands, grateful for quiet,
as waiting for a first gull, or shift of curlew
navigating beyond a pepper scatter of plovers.

Five: I wake on my back, as in a hammock,
light for an hour, now, and a bird's rehearsing
the day, and I look up as in an orchard
with its green sky, lighthouse sunlight; planetary apples.

Six: the other end of a day, and a bell
echoes off mountains, calling the vale to Communion;
each penitent pilgrim navigates runnels and potholes
to a small barn of a church, sheltered by yews.

Seven: we return from the altar and bow our heads,
let words flow as a breeze fills fruit from blossom.
Whether the sermon lingers few will know,
but beyond a wafer, sipped sour wine, a healing.

# Reykjavik

Aiming over the bowl, steadying the phial,
I feel it warming as yellow level rises.
Switch off, screw on the blue top tight,
hope against leak in rucksack into hospital.

Glass on these side street pavements after
overnight sleet; slight skids, taunting of footsteps
sets the pace for morning, uncertainty.

Rest of the world texting, or in free papers
as terraces form avenues to the Metro.
Follow the sketch map past shops, round departments
of the University, track departments A to Z.

After the questions, scales, three phials of blood,
the hand-over; modesty in a yellow carrier
brought during snow in Reykjavik to wrap
a sturdy Viking paperback of sagas.

Snort from the nurse: "Specialists are obsessed
with urine!" First, surgeon, then the ECG,
the nurse, twice, then the anaesthetist.

You want to ask for it back, but saying:
"I like to keep plastic carriers from somewhere
with resonance" seems out of place. Emerging
back into air you find the morning thawed.

## Cycling

Stripped to the waist, masked, patched with tentacles
sagging from chest to a bank of flickering numbers,
I prepare to pedal away, watching the wall,
keeping the handlebar screen between fifty and sixty.

Going nowhere except past a milestone test,
third hospital, uphill towards the operation,
somewhere after Christmas, as through rising hills
of chemotherapy; forecast of shadowed valleys.

"Keep going! Push harder!" Computerised slopes are steepened,
snorkelling to last gasp, monitoring that my heart
is fit enough for incision, small camera, scanning interior.

Some Cumbrian geography, to make you feel at home:
"Like climbing Whinlatter, this last bit!" then the ease
as propping a bike against a boundary stone. Only
outside do you feel free passage of air again.

**Out**


Never been "out" before; now pad in unaccustomed
slippers, once dismissed with the bourgeoisie;
corridors part, white, prints in artificial light,
glimpses, perhaps of Whitley Bay, or somewhere.

You are called into a stilled room , without windows.
Just people and machines, though always kindness;
always a laying down, rehearsed occasions,

dark, though, to those within them; strangers.
And when you wake there are some other bodies
being cleared away. You watch fast-passing ceiling tiles.

After a couple of procedures they let you out.
To ironic Mercedes taxi for this patient city
still there; wide-awake dusk inhaling traffic.
Cirrus on light blue; needle scratch on stained glass.

## Last Orders

Three pips at four-fifteen, pippets continue,
a yellow pulse replaces monitor's gradual
countdown, drip-feed for six hours after
injection of a fluid like thick, dark blood.

A nurse answers my thumb print summoning,
black skirted symbol on a traffic light,
icon for Stop. He turns the piping off,
harvests deflated sac from a metal tree.

Changeover, for a new pouch of clear plastic.
Drips resume, like a slow thaw, through a filter
down the long plastic vein into my arm:
six hours till the final disconnection.

Timetable till Christmas Eve for swallowing
six tablets every day as final helping.
Small war through poisoning, and then a programme
of respite, surgery, respite; the next cycle.

# Countdown

Tablets perhaps about same size as the tumour,
reticent in silver foil, resemble body armour;
inside skin-pink, dissolving in ventilating bubbles.

They are taken out twice a day from a cardboard box
labelled with a yellow warning: "Do not handle if pregnant."

Three swallows, morning and evening, a gulped trinity
of prayers for survival, and a neat tick
on the paper listing countdown to Christmas Eve.

Bible texts tells us you are coming, like a bright star.

We try to imagine shrinkage of threat and miles;
immediate, internal, and closing distance on maps;
the small voice in the book recalling recognition.

We ought to develop a ceremony: save the mug
used each day, for an estimated four hundred and fifty
tablets against one tumour, in the hope of shrinkage.

Last swill and swallow, feel it tilt through the throat,
carry the mug to the fell, inter it in a barrow,
counting back: two, three, four thousand years ago.

## Hungers

Stomach turns like the drain of recycled tea bags,
linger of mince that seems to follow you home
from menus you tick in wards, not wanting
anything offered; just fresh air, your own space.

Life's about losses as the main digestion
becomes that scarlet liquid through the vein,
and ticking the tablet chart. Gradually hair,
some three weeks in, thins; comb thatches it out,

followed by departure of taste, so appetite
turns from appreciation to repulsion. "You
must eat, keep your strength up," knowing
there will be some enforced fasting, after the knives.

Miracle would be to return to favourite places;
that daytime cafe that conjures up Chinese
after six, beamed pubs with open fires,
heavyweight pie and chips: "Choose anything"

at present impossible. Other end of hands
are bamboo arms, thin skin on parchment faces.
Millions will return to sleep without the option
of table, place-setting, cut glass; even hospital menu.

# Rooms

A water colour of Eilean Donan Castle, pencil outlines
still showing through tower and bridge, otherwise
emptiness. Seating for seven, a tea-stained mug,
a poster selling life insurance, and a free pen;
three vacant coat pegs shaped as upended questions.

No voices, just a phone, pleading, unanswered
down an empty corridor, passing squeak of footsteps;
an antiseptic echo now a cleaner's swabbed
grey pathways to side rooms, and recumbent statues
of stands at angles among stacked tubes, fresh linen.

Briefings about fractions of days, leading to months,
six to seven hours in focus in the theatre,
a star billing, perhaps a year of curtain calls,
week or two on wards, that decimal point
of risk outside the forecast of "complete cure".

Tests, bloods, talks, blood pressure, procedure,
that numerical vocabulary of red and green
figures on screens, an approving glance,
"Better than before". A weathering forecast,
storm warning, and curlew calling over moorland.

Returning, a week later, we pause at the garrison's
winded height. Stretched sky snuffs out odd, out-of- season
sunflower sun. Opening the car door threatens to tear
air from air in ancient, pagan shrieking.
Then dip to the city, with its operating theatres.

## Night Flight

Same hissing mystery as overnight, long-haul flight;
lights dimmed into a dusk, dials counting down
hours to arrival, flickering of aerial miles,
drips weeping through high sachets, pulsing light
as wing-tips over cities rest, then dip.

You read a book at thirty-three thousand feet,
probably over Indonesia, local time,
about two-thirty, England, and its cathedrals
on coloured pages, half a world away.

Night spins its own cocoons; a fuselage,
slumped figures or the glow of subdued screens;
hospital ward with soundtrack of coughs or breaths;
each vagrant in space and time; awaiting touchdown.

**Pen**


Street urchin, found on the pavement outside the hospital,
stray biro, high thermometer of black ink,
full enough to draft a white-hot novel, nuclear poems,
something to write home about from the cancer ward.

Does it come loaded with words? In other
hands it might sketch directions, or an ancient face,
scribble a note about leaving, or a luggage list,
or names of those who still need Christmas cards.

Does it wait like an advertised Mass with inbuilt intention?
It could have been meant to add deft calculations
to a maths theory as a scholar went home by bus,
or stand ready, near the heart, for the evening crossword,

having to admit defeat, or have found itself
part of the walker's diary for the Roman wall,
and now city. What is this language that it finds
itself recording in new movements by a different hand?

Small strokes become our spoor, leavings unremarked
unless someone had stooped and thought to bring this in
to where they ask you, gowned, if you'll walk to the theatre.

## Going to the Theatre
## John 21:18

First, a shower, then two gowns, one back
to front, the other front to back, a pair
of slippers: a costume-fitting for the theatre.

We walked: down corridors, as under escort,
a nurse to hand. I had no fear of forgetting
my lines. The stage was set. Things felt prepared.

The surgeon had called in, the anaesthetist,
the evening before to ask me if I knew
what they were going to do. I'd signed disclaimers.

It felt ready; all the rehearsing over,
the months of tablets, hair loss, brief reprieve
when strength returned; assumption of old roles.

I'm turned, sit sideways in the anteroom.
The anaesthetist lifts the back gown covering
my spine, inserts a fine line. Fade.


We've looked forward, to ebb tide after a shower.
Shore's sheened with mingled currents through wormed
shallows,
beach echoes evening sky, sands turned to greys.

We tread a cloud path, watching our footsteps linger
where we chose to print them, as when we were young.
They fill like tears in rain; salt with fresh water.

# Oak

We never had that final conversation.
Your background was always going to clash with mine-
private school, Oxbridge, science, and then theology
you would probably prefer to refer to as Bible Studies.

So better prepared to be always ahead,
your diagnosis confirmed before my time
for clinics, scans, first cycle of chemo-therapy...

You were always one of those who would not come back.
I aired expletives, in private, about shit and pain.
I heard you were much more faithful: 'Trusting the Lord.'

I draft my roles for God watching a cloudbank,
being grey but impotent, devoid of showers:
Adjudicator, Indifferent, Blind Navigator, Prodigal Father.

You would not agree. I remember walking down
to theatre, on the same day as your funeral.

I recalled that, seeing the oak, newly-felled, sliced,
still massive in its components, that part of trunk
that rolled the bank, my height in its cross-section.
So many saw-blade scars, hard to count age rings,

and all around severed arms, meshes of branches,
clues to death in the wither and reach of rot,
and so deep in this wood, far from the track,
likely to become decayed city, and memorial.

Expert on fungii, you'd have mapped its strength
even fallen, potential for resurrection
after decades of lying still, of constant changing.
Debate: between some certainty, and exploration.

# Prayer

Sit jack-knifed on a bed. Feet
ramped on a stool while an anaesthetist
xylophones vertebrae for an appropriate entrance.

Body moulded to something almost Anglican,
somewhere between deference and question-mark;
same fluttering silence while organ's undertones
accompany whispers about readings, coffee rotas.

Silence will hallmark these next seven hours
while those in their own version re-enact
liturgy and sacrifice with gowns, and knives.


Gradually ceiling tiles return to focus, continue
to travel above you over pulses of linoleum,
back to High Dependency Unit's intercessions.

Returning will take a whole pilgrimage of healing,
continuing between the curlew's calling, and the shipping
forecast.

## Operation

You ask what it was like. I barely know.
I remember waiting, being given two plastic gowns
covering back and front, tied into a surgical tabard.

I walked along some corridors under escort
as if to receive an award, or perform something;
same sense of anticipation, almost confrontation;
that passing through open doors, normally closed.

I remember sitting sideways on a bed
while they opened the gown at the back to probe the spine,
to enter the epidural. They showed me the line,
afterwards, even thinner than angler's nylon.

Invitation to breathe something, and next
moment white tiles are re-forming on the ceiling.
Abstracts of them, as the bed was steered out
under jarred angles, discontinuity and overlap.

From what I heard afterwards, something of breaking and
entering,
a spare rib loosed or sawed, right arm twisted
out of the way in a gesture of surrender.
Incisions, connecting tubes; snake-charming of gut.

Shrunk tumour difficult to find, then stitching,
disconnecting an octopus of tubes, then someone ringing:
'He's awake again, and really seems quite perky.
You can come in, if you like. It's gone to plan.'

# Nails

Nails came early; a good three months before
most Easters. Anaesthetic to pin you down,
a theatre's array of scalpels; cutting gear.

A different shape from traditional cruciform:
flat on your back, one arm reportedly angled
out of the way. Still a spear in the side.

Same darkness, also, between moments of capture
and coming round from wherever you had been.
No memory, just a refocussing. There, tiles

squaring the ceiling; there, presumably, a rising
sun, shape of an eclipsed stone rolled aside;
there, a liana of tubes, like garden tendrils.

Here, up on our feet, as dew tingling bare soles
nailed limp, and a rusty after-taste; sponged vinegar.

## Scale

'Tell me where the pain is, on a scale
of one to ten.' Day after the operation,
spear in the side: 'About eight'.

Morphine; a resurrection breathing exercise
settles it. Weeks later, in another bed,
the spearhead fades to an ache of three or four.

Difficult to quantify, defining ache or pain,
subjective thresholds. A woman dissolved in grief
makes television news just before Easter.

Her robes same Mary blue. We do not know
her name, only massacre context, Kenya,
as distant in place as Palestine in time.

Crown of thorns, on a scale of one to ten?
Nail through the wrist, edging towards a nine?

# Visitation

The chaplain came as pilgrim, empty-handed;
no staff, pack, spare coat, sandals for the road;
no book, or scripted prayers; just question marks.

We circled. I told her my wife had been ordained.
She underlined her role as permanent deacon,
but asked if we could talk; drew up a chair.

I must have been trussed up and octopussed
with tubes and piping. She must have worn her name
on a badge between her collar, and a modest cross.

Her questions easy: Why was I here? How long?
I wanted to ask about the role of God,
creator and/or redeemer of disease?

And who had done that theological homework?
Where did belief and cancer co-exist?
Had Lazarus died of it? Why miracles silent

of its cure, or even presence? And had it come
only with the nuclear bomb, disguised as power?
Was illness other end of nuclear fuse

that first day of creation? A staff nurse came
needing to do something private, within drawn curtains,
leaving the chaplain's conversation backlit.

We did not meet again. Tonight thick cloud snuffs out red bars of winter sunlight. When might chance come to re-phrase questions again?

## Gloves

Blue plastic crackles, changed to second hands
as gloves are plucked from boxes, small to large,
peeled to the wrist, become a second skin
to handle what is healing, intimate.

Sometimes to draw blood, rinse the feeding tube,
prise home a suppository with appropriate pardon:
"Excuse me", inject ("Sharp scratch"), complete
the morning wash beyond reach, ("the lower parts").

Same colour as sky in Mediterranean frame,
hot blue inseparable from a bathing sea,
fantasy unrolled as if completing journey
world away from grey swathe of a Tyneside winter

seen through high windows overlooking a crossing.
Foot pedal prises high bin's clang of lid,
gloves rippled loose, dropped in, clutching at air
that will retain close memories; healing, kindness.

## Learning to Walk

Resuming beginnings; you rise reluctantly
as once obeying historic calls to anthems,
or adding hallelujah to a chorus, stand
while the world simmers, then steadies underfoot.

Notch three fingers under a ledge on the drip-feed trolley.
The physio lifts two pails among festooning wires.
You set off like a maypole, taking it slowly,
one step at a time, as totter decades ago.

Escort defines geography; a route  in angles
down corridors, small views are window-framed
re-connecting the ordinary, modest hiker glancing
at flower beds shut for winter, then the stadium
silent between matches: name-plates across closed doors.

Progress will mean abandoning machines,
letting them fall away like space-craft stages,
waving farewell to supporters, attempting stride,
recalling how our Cumbrian ridge supports wild stars.

## Corridor

He appeared strangely, far end of the hospital corridor
otherwise empty, seeming a mile away,
shadowing each panel of sunlight as staining glass,
but silently. We expected no word from him.

Suddenly no-one there; "without a prayer"
in the vernacular, distance and absence shared,
and we pressed on, the physio at my right hand
to steady the distance, aiming for the slight ramp.

Incline into future; the next prayer
the retired priest discusses. "No longer there
asking for anything; just welcoming, presence".

Gale all night, rattle-sticked hail on pane;
that reminder, in pained dark, of story
of wind and fire sent out to change the world.

No rings, no haloes of flame before first light,
but sigh in air of absence and remembering:
the kind hand waiting at elbow, in case of falter.

## Osaka

Sleep comes as stranger, at strange hours,
with aches and pains and antidote of medication
turning the usual timetable to discussion.

So, four am., between blood pressure and morphine,
becomes evening for headphones bringing music,
or reading, or sitting propped in daffodil light

remembering an alarm clock, years ago,
trilling at that time, ready for the airport taxi,
then early flight to Frankfurt, then Osaka.

Arrival now is not a man-made island
we'd scratched half-world of skies to marvel at,
but reaching for a hazel stick to steady steps,

and interview not a magnate's evasive answers
but echo of woodpecker probing trunk for feeding,
and outlook not a thousand vehicles arching

skyline over miles of overpass,
silent through triple-glazing, but slow fall
of fields to woods, and sea ruled straight above them.

Journey is no longer far, but re-defining
nearness into a re-examined wonder
as all the familiar's magicked, and made strange.

Somewhere in Japan, a far more ancient discipline
than merely designing airports, counting yen
would equally hear old language of light on stone.

## Back in Place

Landscape is back in place after journey home,
time of arrival fanfared in barred gold,
unravelled sky is skeined like an open fire.

Outlook fades; from sea, trees, to near-fields.
Dusk drains down greens to blacks, and smoke-cured grey.
Cottage fits to the fell, is interlocked.

Time is remembering what we passed as landmarks:
high ground's spined ridge edge along the Roman wall;
Vallum fur-lined with snow, copse drilled as if

legion became woodland, patrol and sentinel.
Low scarecrow copses lean back to our speed;
then sky breaks over mountains we can name.

Here buzzard has kept faith, sieving through wings
rounds of air, fingering spirals as she rises,
keening for all that's lost, in all its gathering

as writers watch out over wintering country
(travel with them for a word, MacCaig in Assynt,
Longley who walks the lyric over machair).

Each writes from borrowed ground, an adopted room,
knows that return is simply antiphon
to what the silence sang, during our absence.

## Climber

Each stair a different shape; first step an oblong
rising to triangle, diamond at the turn
between hall and landing; an ascending geometry lesson.

Once climbed without thinking, but since the operation
a shuffle, gasped steps, different weight of effort,
best foot forward, then a pause, a pause
for the other to catch up, repeat; no fluency.

Next step will be to rise as if attaining air,
counting up one to ten, the steadying rail
gripped, and transferring where the oblong light
guides final pitch, right-angled to the landing.

Feel carved globe under your palm after ascent,
similar in its grain to the gate up to the fell.
We lift our eyes to the hills, and plan to follow.

## Travel Section

We are told to "lie still", just in case
a cannula's wrenched by movement from a vein.
So we're flat on our backs like an exhausted banker
waiting for cocktails under expensive sunlight.

New Year arrives with brochures; a new cruise
could take you to the Arctic while below
saltwater line the waiters dream of home
advertised elsewhere for its starred hotels.

Each destination seems to start with flight:
Gatwick, Heathrow to safari, classic Greece.
The Berlin Tour includes a prison camp,
the Vietnam trip some 'fascinating' war-zone tunnels.

The man, stretched as in sunlight, reminisces
across the ward: "They gave me eighteen months;
that got me to Dubrovnik". Overhead
chalk vapour trails draft warnings of global warming.


This journey starts with views from a four-bed ward,
of pimpled hail cupped in sycamore leaf, continues
with blush of retiring cloud, polish of wind
as path turns through the woods, a creak of beech

uneased by threat of gale. From hospital grounds,
after starting a second round of chemotherapy,
we turn home before snow. The globe aches.

## Second Cycle

Black bag like a Tudor executioner's hood
covers a clear pouch hoisted over my head.

I am victim and patient, subject to contraband,
tied by the plug leeched to the back of my hand

by bandage and tape, freed by drip-feed
with poison that searches throughout my body and blood

defining the plot against escapee, rogue cell,
as crack in the wall, tear in the veil.

Role: watchman over a darkening view
where rough grass levels to brick walls, windows, roofs

out to grey Pennine ridge-tile and thatched sky,
and briefly geese, arrowing to estuary.

They will soon turn North, for Spring, begin to follow,
blood-line, clear liquid blebbing into thaw,
same line as dark vein that pulses into me.

## A Patient Opposite

Vertical view framed in a hospital window,
lower quarter a slow dance of dithering leaves
fresh green in late Spring. The rest a quietening sky

like duvet pulled over slowly. Wind sinks after a storm.
Spread iron puddles reflect a twitter of swifts
hunting against cloudbank. Spread gulls dry their wings.

Stand, and you overlook barriers of trees,
and catch same greys drying among Scottish hills,
rinsed wool between dyeing and weave, before colouring.

A patient opposite compares notes about dressings,
his long haul through infections, a farmer friend who
had a return, denying lambing, harvest.

Later, check light through curtain and plastic slat;
tree's sketched by a lamp, high lime and then black shadow.
Ten; there's still wait in the light, matching ward's stillness
after conversations, unsettling of unfinished business.

## Source


Impossible to conjure such deep darkness
as in the Genesis story. Only by standing
blindfold in mid-Atlantic, overhearing turmoil
of crest and trough, might you begin to approach it.

Here, if we look to the sea, levelled
over a scatter of hamlet lights, nothing
shows among fields and woods except
one glow, like a downed star, out, along west's coastline.

That, and the orange smear to the North
of the atomic bomb factory, or cancer town,
or safety zone, depending on interpretation;
perpetual light of an inverted constellation.

Seen also from the fell road, where circled stones
ring mystery stretching  back to the Biblical.
And same old questions tremble up there also
like cotton grass in Spring wind, their tufts white

against each darkening sky: Who was it formed
the cancer cell, loosed it to work
among us, as a symbol of malice, hate,
or, in creation, blinked, or abdicated?

## Borders

Looking back, you find that this stage of the journey,
is coast to coast, back to back, Irt to Tyne,
but turning off before that official route,
taking the fell well south of St Bees' start.

Then meeting it round a ring of ancient stones,
following it downhill, bidding it farewell
as it burrows into Ennerdale, and we keep North,
circling mountains, seeking the Romans' roads

east, as you might listen out for curlew,
their overflow of water on chilled wind,
here before land was ruled into division,
stone squared to boundary; soldiers with new gods.

Not that long since it seems, as wind still harries
high distance sharpening sunlight's definition
of history over moors, an upper world;
only the soundtrack's changed; legions, then motorists.

Arc: diagnosis, tests, same lifting journey,
struggle to rise within the chemotherapy,
pause at the watershed of operation,
more chemo as downhill to farthest coast.

Today, just words; no needles, tubes or cannulas,
returning as the city draws its sentry cloak
tighter; miles longer now, borders mysterious.

## Revision Course

Beginning again by going back to woods
means changing the angle of walk from level to incline,
leaning into the strain where the rib was fractured,
leaning into pain when trip jars footstep.

Third leg of stick punts down the gouged-out track
washed back to rungs of tree roots by last winter,
takes hike in its stride where needles soften footfall,
pauses at felled oak's cross-section of generations.

Higher, and you are within language of trees,
larch tapering creak to whispered myth of ocean,
music among fallings, requiems, violin tunings,
bristle and rustle of beech that keeps leaves wintered.

I try to remember words for Spring among them,
pause by the boulder wall with its pelt of moss,
rehearing what recent centuries would have told us,
when footsteps pause; vocabulary, revision course.

# Creed

A radio programme discusses with mathematicians
how they offer proof, thinking through weeks and months,
covering pages with equations, showing the working.

They start from where they are; self, number one,
setting their minds to the elegance of others'
equations, something almost theologically mysterious,
like waking after surgery, wondering where you've been.

You are left, spared, survivor, though a marionette
with tubes everywhere, perhaps a couple of years
before you are "right again", and in a different form;
theorem re-written, basically, from first principles.

Double negative: it is not that I do not believe
in God, but how good a father was he, how
almighty when the cancer cell was formed?

And not that I do not know, and try to follow
Jesus Christ, only Son, our Lord and healer.
But did his father blink, or abdicate
that moment of low blood count, birth of tumour?

Trinity of questions. It is not the Holy Spirit
that I doubt, but how "the lord and giver of life"
might have missed a trick in calculus and working out,
equalling the glory due to father and son.

We are left with subtractions- the holy catholic church?
Writing is freelance, rather than institutional-
communion of saints?- we remain first person, singular,
like the mathematician; his blank sheet examining infinity.

## Silage

Everything striped, from garden shed's overlaps
to red and yellow labels on the baler
gathering silage, squaring cut turquoise lines.

For two, three days the field's been bars of grass
seen from the air, from the wild track to the fell,
sliced and turned for drying before forecast rain.

Then engine through the peace, a careful steer
to suck, collect; roll up to clear and bale,
as rubbing back a painting to its founding canvas.

Outsiders come, from coastlines, pointillist gulls,
not normally seen till heralds of storm warning,
now white dots on lined lime, a gleaning horde.

I also silage: reveal with shears old stones
marking a border in this wandering garden;
gather felled grass to heat, and fade to compost,

and run my fingers over shortened stalks,
felling their stubble like prickles on chin and cheeks
that hint of growth, in weeks after last tablets.

## Punctuation

Across the pillow, like punctuation marks-
commas, halved semi-colons, tops of questions-
hairs curl without any commentary or comment:

no text or lists, nothing requiring pauses,
or possibilities of answers. Blacker
than hair before chemo, its initial shedding.

Small scratches across blue cotton, as if rehearsing
structure where essay, thesis or poem might follow,
and now a second shedding; next revision

filling in blanks, hoping for what might follow:
"You must be better- your curls are coming back.
It's not the same, but soon you'll you need a hair-cut."

Vanity project? Yet part of our defining
ourselves, a comb and length to follow, protest;
and off the top of our heads an autobiography.

## Bouquet

Last sunlight turns Azalea into a bride,
inherent yellow being her own bouquet;
a slight sigh on the breeze her wedding night.

Similar to the withdrawal of the gift set tube,
plumbed straight through stomach into abdomen;
flat plastic circle stitched into the skin,
dangling connector like a beer keg valve

that nozzles into a pipe out of the pump,
that chugs in nutrients ten hours every night.
Nine inches of line drawn out, skin sealed with dressing.

Back in the garden, first time for six months,
able to bend without fear of stab or wrench;
so mind's loose, seeing white as sacrament,
and everywhere as evidence of gifts.

# Prodigal

I return to the hospital room not knowing
where I have been. The clear pipe breathing oxygen
has been removed, whatever was veining my arm
has stopped flowing. The screen mapping my interior
is blank again. The short sedation has been realised.

Recently a probe has followed the route of my throat
while I was elsewhere. Silently, painlessly,
while my identity was a named bracelet
on my left wrist. The good news is that it found
nothing untoward. Triumph is in absence.

Kind nurses whose names I have forgotten
help me to my feet, tell me I must not drive,
or operate machinery for twenty-four hours.
Had I been there I would have seen a coating
of many colours pulsing deep space of my interior.

Feet on the ground again, I wait for escort,
love that will take me home, having survived
months of treatment- chemo, surgery, chemo,
and a walking frame, becoming more fluent than crutches.

The waiting-room windows with their porthole glass
reduce passers-by to fractions of themselves.
I watch from inside, not allowed back into the world
by myself in case of after-shock, side effects.
I return as coming to home ground from a far country
having been restored, somehow made whole by absence.

## Calendar

Turn pages slowly across these Scottish islands,
Harris and Lewis, both Uists, Barra, Skye,
each given a month; boundaries of ground and ocean.

Also the journal, half-page or thereabouts,
small space to leave a day, usually written
from end point close to midnight, edge of morrow.

And each month, day, progress with question-marks.
Often same formula, hours slept, new times of rising;
meals, walking managed, short journeys in the car

as passenger, still; still weak at clutch and brake.
So all the more ironic to find The Quairaing,
viewpoint for the Trottenish Ridge that spines East Skye

gained only with fit legs, and head for heights.
Pause here by tangled thorn in autumn's palette,
spread ferrous bracken, lemons and lichen's limes

and let the healing parable translate
from the original into tomorrow's language,
like turning a Gaelic dictionary, page by page.

**Ticking the Script**


Limpets on legs, arms, stomach, an octopus
clipped to plastic tags: "Lie very still,"
on the clinic couch. The machine whirs
like a submarine's propeller at full fathom five.

Paper glides, blunted serpent's tongue,
its message coded for experts to decide
what happens next , like a playwright with an island
and how it fits with magic, and a shipwreck.

Things to come: further scan, consultations:
"Not expecting anything; just wanting to be sure."
Still those words on the last page, hopeful: "complete cure".

Later we go to the coast, air charged with salt,
white crests, clear North to St Bees Head, on to Galloway.
Three letters, E-C-G, ticked off the script.

## October

"Nothing to be done": a white cube of a room-
more cubicle than room- no road, tree, evening,
but an afternoon injunction: "Just relax".

Sole object of waiting, wax jacket hung on the door,
an overflow of tallow from a gutted frame,
cavity of a hood, sag of frayed plaid.
Coat just about hanging on by a wispy loop.

"Time passes." Click and shudder of an uncertain door.
An invitation to lie on a sheet of paper.
A door closes again, tube clamps like a mask,
and a grey line, inches from eyes, becomes horizon.

Shunted in, you become the vein of the stationary vehicle.
Close eyes to award more space, count down the time.
Eventually you see clear sky in the form of ceiling,
then numbers flicker, reversing time to freedom.

Voice broadcasts from next room: "The scan's complete."
Wedge slid from behind your knees, gradually upright
you let the unit settle before you move;
spaceman, find your feet, return to gravity.

Hands in pockets re-connect. Your house key,
notebook with its unturned pages, pen to hand,
cracked wax now ready for the wood's brush with bent leaves,
to hear wind ravel beech boughs. Rain's forecast.

# Navigator

Blackout in mid-Atlantic; roll-call in yellow, red
of emergency lighting, so many mispronounced
Filipino names. There is barely a wind.

The chief officer found him, the blindfolded navigator,
feeling his way along varnished rails leprous with sea-spray.
'Now we are dependent solely on the stars.'

There appeared to be no motive for the attack,
nothing in his health records or background,
no correlations as between smoking and lungs.

What made it such a shock to a healthy life?
Who was on night watch as the tumour grew?
Who expressed love as chemo-vomit, or probing scalpel?

All we could do was stand in salted darkness
trying to remember training. Someone recalled
only the navigator knew hours of dawns, of tides.

# Frame

Almost a matching silver to the sea as we look west,
late afternoon aluminium, same sort of framework
as rucksack backpack; same sort of plastic grip
as walking poles. Frame set for stand-up.

Element of comedy at my age, yet also
relief or blessing that injury was 'stable fracture'.
Angle it back to a rear of rubber hooves
then heave into surround that's grounded, stable,

and best foot forward to the base camp hall.
Park. Reach for the new rail at the turn
of stripped wooden bannisters, undamaged ankle
taking lead on each step, hands foraging forward

to take weight, skew body up through effort, angle.
Sometimes a smooth rise as finding right route up rock;
sometimes a gasped trial up ragged, cragged expletives.
Handhold on top bannister; final haul; love's contact.

## Ash Wednesday

Scattered, they gather to speak against the disease,
to exercise whatever they mean by prayer,
sometimes a candle, or a woodland walk,
a name added to a pause within a liturgy.

They are better apart; the woman who does not "do
religion", and the Calvinist; bands within the Anglican
rainbow.
Those outside the church, those pillaring its establishment,
those who no longer attend, but retain "a something",
perhaps finding echo in quiet pleas for healing.

They come to Ash Wednesday like an overhearing,
reminded by news of surgery, convalescence,
of wilderness and temptation, perhaps the mystery

a poet wrung from it, that same potential for searching
through words planted where night is pared by lightning:
each person who names my name, besides their own.

**Hoy**


Mindfulness exercise: you track weight
from crown to sole, and register support,
then let the breaths take charge, counting out life.

Think kindness, as a currency or gift,
imagine those in need, and welcome them,
conjure them, even, so they sit before you,
details you recognise; poise, bearded smile;
bring them into that shelter, out of conflict.

Mind wanders, out to Orkney, out to Hoy,
the military museum, dense tonnage of it;
everything in cold black steel, a bicycle
a paratrooper took, or left behind;
everything built of burden; shell cases, field guns.

End of day: streaming weather when names were read,
a silence kept, a kindness to past pain.
Dusk brings an easing to the drumhead downpour,
sky's broken open like an oyster shell.
We rise, and put on boots, and venture out.

## Airports

Small cymbals draped over a hand are chimed
to tingling echoes, taking seconds to fade,
as entry into mindfulness is gently opened.

Perception's grounded in soles, and filters upwards
through legs and chest- no mention of the heart-
to arrive at the crown of head, as poised for take-off.

The mind is allowed to wander, then summoned back,
gently, for the whole exercise is kindness
flowing through like a beck. Mind
                                        slips to airports,

strangers' places, where nobody belongs,
one end of a destination, departure lounge,
air thunderous with overcrowding, rattle-bag soundtrack,

cut-pricing and overcharging, spotlit economy,
anxiety tinged with spread-eagled liberation;
whole world potential in a constant shuffle of place-names.

"And bring the mind gently back." Glass walkways
where people tow lives as miming through aquaria.
Hear cymbals' tingled echoes; feel arms becoming wings.

## Theologian

His desk was the stormed beech, a kind wood
felled by a lightning trident, tongued and grooved
to spread three widths of foolscap, yesterday's

notes, progress, memos, blank surface for today,
and elbowing in the eternal writing hand.
He'd brought the loosed length home, after the fall.

Part barked with crisping skin, but also sheered
to underwood, direction of brown, white grain;
part flow, a river and a zebra skin,

part matt, and partly polished, partly shined.
He noted rasp of snap, fracture where branch
had left length wounded like departed bone.

Given craft, he'd inlay, gouge channel for pens,
or like a relic in a consecration,
placed in an altar, sealed with blade and mortar.

That day's page blank, till he interrogated
branch, bark and grain, and, walking back into woodland,
noticed how boughs had bent back bark to beckoning.

## Night Shift


Black duffel coat hangs from the door like a dead
crow, though arms at attention rather than splayed
wings of a bird strung after shotgun crucifixion.

Past its best; hem never the same after
mice nibbled it in an empty house, lashings on toggles
sagged and hamstrung after storms; nap sheened

by campaigns against weather and thorned gardening.
Pockets still intact for glasses, and notebook to check
types of owl in torchlight, lapwings in starlight.

The nurse asks about hours of sleep. You confess
a twelve hour night, with restlessness till four.
She labels it a night shift, matt-black without moon.

One night you will wear the coat to the sands;
listen there for whatever wild cries out.

## Half-mile

Half-mile through beech woods to the River Irt,
from road along the track to the crook-backed bridge,
half-circle over beck, barely a cart's width.
Path, recently fettled with gravel, original, before tarmac.

Now journey is out through weather, as well as light
turning down like an oiled wick, leaving field
first, then edging scree to Dutch caps of snow
above two thousand contours. All the while

echo of wind from shelter. Victorian hems
rustling through hedge leaves that wait for Spring to scatter.
Two young trees lopped by gale defy fall at angle,
and walk is through mast, scripted manuscript bark,

and turn where felling's made a second bridge.
That day's achievement, and the half-mile back,
rehearsal for those high places gathering darkness.

**Edge**


Low tide; a mile along the beach I seek
a flat stone as a seat before returning,
a granite slab that's come out of the sea,
or down the dale, speed of withdrawing glacier.

Wedge, perch, take moments just to re-assess
the familiar; how dark tongues of stone go seeking
to bridge sands onto water, how sound's frilled
as tide turns and returns, how plover, dunlin

gradually re-appear as pepper specks, given detail,
to probe where foreshore's damped by reaching shallow;
to guess the height and reach of rampart dunes.

Perhaps we are alone? Another figure might walk,
miles away, as distance ebbs out to sea's edge.
Having sat, I rise; then make my own way back.

# Catch

Some stayed so short a time their days
were numbered on stone in little years and months
between broad foreshore and those first quiet fields.
Among clanned churchyard names one "Lost in the snow".

I bring the mug that swilled fat tablets down,
its own words name of a town, an invitation
to learn more in third age, that of survivors.

That medicine almost done, I seek loose stone
to add it to the burials above the sea's
whisper, and oyster catchers' pips of piping.

No give in ground, there's a lock on the dead.
I climb the ladder stile, feel shingle give
small landslides under footfall, find some net
blue against turf, reed, sunned marsh marigold,
a crumpled landfall from the weekend storm.

I prise strands loose, slip in the mug as catch.

## Afterlight

Sea-angler pauses, casts out as we pass
on the slow train edging towards a coffee morning
next day, a world away, an opposite river.

Change. Owl-eye siding lights blink through stripped beeches;
quick, ripped-off names shred non-stop country stations;
Christmas lights semaphore off white-washed gables;
boulder walls, fields retreat to after-light.

Next morning hundreds; convention of survivors.
Raffle as you enter, baking, stalls of knitting;
those archive page scents, flowers, crowds, fresh coffee,

then silence for the videos of former patients
who scaled Three Peaks, cantered The Great North Run.
Touches on arms, smiles of half-recognition
from nursing staff who loaned their lives to ours.

Still grateful for hand-railed stairs back to the station;
long journey of recovery after knives,
skilled as assassins', teased the tumour out.

Still light as train grinds back towards the watershed
rising above trees as rolling out a map
of all North's moorland. Promise where the estuary
refines the silver early-closing evening.

Ermine of new snow collars the Roman Vallum;
then coffee stall at lightfall, changing trains;
then the request stop, where you chose a homecoming.

## After Curlew   (from *Curlew Moon* by Mary Colwell)

In memory and memorial, track and trace
birdwatcher boot-steps following five hundred miles
cross Ireland, across England, seeking curlew.

Not always what she expected, habitat
destroyed by peat extraction, Celtic moorlands
silent; too early mowing of hay meadows.

Theft-depth of wild grass curlew need for nesting,
paradox of conservation guarding predators,
need to draft new alliance between yields and gunmen.

She also missed a turning, kept too straight
arrow through Wales, missing the Northern note
along the wintering Solway, Cumbrian coast,

lament and consolation in one song.
(As for the friend, who copied from a watcher's print
the pebbled chest and pickaxe probe of bill,

whom we remember now her music's spent.
Life-wish and death-wish for salt coasts, linged moorlands
we honour in the painting kindness gave.)

As hand, steadying on sands, an overhearing,
sharp piping and long glide of Latin name;
hope for a time of sky-shared piccolo

defining them by absence, as endangered species,
as presence beyond identity, faith beyond creed.
They are followers of the old ways, as we would track

North, to hear whaup over loch as evening's calling,
as we would stop to print snow, going home,
following the Roman wall back, after surgery.

Dark would not bring her back, but wait
for light, and the summoning of Spring,
and you might hear, through tide-turn, over moorland,
curlew.

## Visible Music

Each footstep takes us further into deep past,
leaving the tarmac road for the farming gravel
till it runs to grass, well-trodden to prehistory
where some might shed their shoes, sensing ground holy.

Moor drafts succeeding language, gathered wildness,
world rimmed by lope of ridges, glimpse of ocean.
In circles, shafts of stone, monolith signposts
predict cathedral cities' spires and cloisters.

Prophecy, then, that three tall stones should shadow
five thousand years as mother, son and spirit;
or tomb, globed like the world, should hold a body
coiled in a slabbed womb like a question-mark?

Rumours and over-hearings: visible music
is scored through harp-stringed sedge or noted down
where sea-wind song-lines through a boulder wall.
Quick crochet notes re-phrase starched cotton grass.

Curlew's concerto grants a gift of tongues,
its notes quick-quick before its rubbled stream
reveals low profile, fleet, as summoning rain.
Now, like those earlier people with their settling ards,
some time to stand, and some to move away.

**Answer**


Barely the sickle blade of a new moon
reaping thin light behind museum glass,
bone scooped from tideline, plucked out of a moor,
curlew's bill, unsung in converted chapel.

Perhaps become part of the woman's song in the kirk
where she was greeted as stranger, and did not stay
for the holiness, but offered before first hymn
fragment out of her islands, phrased in Gaelic,

and as she came to the chorus, soft as down,
perhaps of the coming barnacle geese, or snow,
those lining the pitch pine pews who shared her language
joined in, as offering flight back to the whaups' skulls.

Wise preacher, he set her free with the bless of a hand,
and later, turning to troubled ripples of psalms,
asked hearers lining plain pews and holy walls:
'What is your song?', and 'How does it begin?'

Waiting to cross to the priory at low water
we heard the curlews' music, answering him.

## Biography

Martyn Halsall grew up in Southport, then in Lancashire, before studying at the College of St Mark and St John, then in Chelsea, at the end of the 'Swinging Sixties'.

After reporting for local and regional newspapers he joined The Guardian as a staff correspondent, specialising first in religious affairs then Northern industry.

He later worked as a communications adviser in the Church of England, and continued postgraduate creative writing studies at the Universities of Lancaster and Cumbria.

His awards include winning three times the Jack Clemo Memorial Competition, and being short-listed in the Keats-Shelley and Manchester Cathedral poetry competitions.

His first full collection, *Sanctuary*, (Canterbury Press) reflected his year as the first Poet in Residence at Carlisle Cathedral, and he has also published five poetry pamphlets.

He lives and writes in rural West Cumbria.

## Notes and Acknowledgements

Thanks are due to the editors of *abridged, faithINITIATIVE,* and *Theology* where some of these poems first appeared.

*Answer* first appeared as Church Music in *Borrowed Ground* (Cylch Cerrig Press: 2018, re-printed 2019).

A version of *Hay Meadow* first appeared in *After Woodland* (Cylch Carrig Press: 2019). The poem draws on references to Jeremiah 28, and to *Curlew Moon* by Mary Colwell (William Collins: 2018).

*Going to the Theatre*: takes reference from John 21:18.

*Oak* was also first published in *About Woodland*. It is dedicated to Steven, 'presbyter'.

*Back in Place*: The Scottish poet Norman MacCaig was frequently inspired by the landscape of Assynt in North-west Scotland. The Irish poet Michael Longley includes frequent references to the machair, coastal hinterland fertilised by wind-blown shell fragments, as on the coast of County Mayo.

*After Curlew*: a whaup is a Scots-Gaelic name for the curlew.

*Visible Music*: an ads is a primitive form of plough, used by ancient peoples as hunter-gatherers became settlers and agriculturalists some 4,500 years ago.

The cover watercolour painting (*Numenius arquata : Curlew*) is by Hilary Meadows.

Dozens of people are involved in the care of any cancer patient, including medical and counselling professionals, family and friends. I would like to thank all those at the following hospitals who contributed to my treatment; their technical skill and compassionate kindness were an equally valued part of the healing process:

West Cumberland Hospital, Whitehaven; Cumberland Infirmary, Carlisle; Royal Victoria Infirmary (RVI), Newcastle upon Tyne; Freeman Hospital, Newcastle upon Tyne, and the Royal Preston Hospital, Preston, Lancashire.

Encouragement from Macmillan Cancer Support during convalescence was greatly appreciated.

And to Isobel, Anna and Rachel, and to Mollie and David for your love and faith, this collection is equally dedicated.

*Numenius arquata: Curlew* by Hilary Meadows.

# Visible Music

CALDEW PRESS

caldew-press@outlook.com

caldewpress.com

Martyn Halsall's previous poetry collections include:

*Sanctuary*, reflecting on a year as the first Poet in Residence at Carlisle Cathedral: Canterbury Press, 2014.

*Coronach*: Wayleave Press, 2016.

*Borrowed Ground*: Cylch Cerrig Press, 2018, re-printed 2019.

*About Woodland*: Cylch Cerrig Press, 2019.

*Passing Place*: Cylch Cerrig Press, 2020.

Printed in Great Britain
by Amazon

80042090R00058